Midhurst WW2 Memoirs:
An Evacuee's Story

Cover: The author with his Dad in mid-1940. The Blitz had not yet started on London.

Midhurst WW2 Memoirs:
An Evacuee's Story

A companion guide to the Midhurst WW2 Memoirs Project

by

Peter H Sydenham

Red Robin Publishing Co. Ltd.

First Published 2018
Red Robin Publishing Pty Ltd
8 Weemala Crescent
Rostrevor
South Australia 5073
Tel: + 61 8 8336 1959
Email: sydenham@senet.com.au
Web: www.midhurstmemoirs.com

Copyright © 2018 Peter Sydenham
All rights reserved. No reproduction permitted
without prior permission of the copyright holders

**Midhurst WW2 Memoirs:
An Evacuee's Story**

ISBN 978-0-6481713-3-1

Printed on Demand by Ingrams

Disclaimer
The publisher of this book has made every effort to ensure the accuracy of the information contained in it but such accuracy cannot be guaranteed. If errors have nevertheless crept in, the publisher apologises, but cannot accept liability for loss of inconvenience resulting from inaccurate information.

Preface

The Midhurst WW2 Memoirs project covers the history of the beautiful Midhurst Rural District up to, and including WW2. The project is intended to be a living research resource for others to pick up from if they seek to delve deeper, or to learn of their heritage.

The project began with my children, and then their children, asking me to help them with their school work on 'What did your father (or grandfather) do in WW2?' Those simple exercises made me realise I only had a superficial child's knowledge of my formative years as an evacuee taken to the Midhurst. That was not good enough!

I initially aspired to prepare a book about my own evacuation experience; it was soon clear it would barely cover 80 pages! It shouldn't take long!

However, I felt it would not contribute much of general interest; but it did lead me to revealing and researching the many back stories behind my own experiences of that time. Fascinating!

This book is the companion guide to the Midhurst WW2 Memoirs series of books. It first gives my own story presented in Midhurst in 2014 to the Midhurst Society, and then describes the follow-on from that event as the books are born.

All books will be made available as Print on Demand editions, along with their e-book equivalents. Local, off the shelf, purchase will be available throughout the Midhurst Rural District.

Keep in touch on www.midhurstmemoirs.com

Based on a
Midhurst Society presentation
by P H Sydenham,
given in the
Cowdray Hall, Midhurst
February 201

What luck - I got Midhurst!

Abstract.

The bombing blitz on London was at its peak. With her only son, Peter, myself, Vi Sydenham took a train to Midhurst in late 1940. I was just 3½yrs old.

It was to be the start of a great adventure for me starting with small country town life, but living without my mum in a billet in the St Ann's Hill building. I started primary education at the Convent school. This was my home until Sheep Lane got bombed in 1943.

A move to Uphams House in Easebourne Street provided me with the rural life experience, albeit mixed with soldiers and lacking running water or electricity in our cottage home.

Then it was back to town life in Red Lion Street, living in a tiny shop. I experienced army parades and fetes, learned that my dad's hut in RAF Kidbrooke London had taken a direct hit by a Doodle Bug. I also stayed for a while in the Fitzhall Gate Lodge.

I enjoyed my time there, but it had to come to an end. In 1945, with Mum, I returned to London to live again with my dad. A few years later we three migrated to Australia.

What Luck - I got Midhurst!

Talk to Midhurst Society
by
Peter Sydenham

WW2 evacuee to Midhurst and Easebourne

Cowdray Hall
Midhurst
11 February 2014

Ladies and Gentlemen.

G-Day from Australia. I hope my mix of London and Aussie accent is understandable. I have been told it has a hint of Midhurst accent.

May I introduce to you Marjorie, my evacuee cousin who is here today from Cambridge. Also, with us from London is Barry Hinton, whose mother and aunt were evacuees here.

I would like to thank the Midhurst Society for this invitation. It is great to be part of the 'Midhurst in Living Memory' project. As I walk around it is hard to take it in that I actually lived in Midhurst and Easebourne some 74 years ago.

So many places here carry memories for me. Perhaps I have romanticised them over the years but they have formed a truly happy formative part of my life. This hall, as the Easebourne Institute in WW2, has a special place in my story; but more on that later.

Mum and Dad's Wedding day, 1935
(Own photo)

Mum (Vi) and Dad (Henry) were married in London in 1935. Dad was a Messenger in the Royal Exchange Assurance REA, next door to the Bank of England. It was a responsible, but poorly paid post.

Crystal Palace in SE London before 1936
(footballheritage.wordpress.com)

In November 1936 the magnificent Crystal Palace in London was burning down. Mum, then 6 months pregnant with me, was there watching it. She must have thought it was the most frightening blaze she could ever imagine. However, another onlooker, Winston Churchill, knew better: he understood war was coming and that it would be horrific for millions of people.

The 1930s was a time of great global tension. Hitler had shown what he was really like - the domination of his ideas by totally inhuman brutality. Thankfully, our family did not fare too badly by the experience: just three men injured, each with a bad leg wound.

1938 Drawing of Hitler playing a pipe organ, as people in the background are being tortured;
(Wikipedia; Images)

By 1938, Hitler's territorial ambitions and oppression were seen for what they were about: the creation a glorious Third Reich, and murdering those he decided should not part of it.

The Time Magazine gave him a 'Man of the Year' cover for 1938 - as the man who was the most infamous. The cover, drawn by a Catholic priest, was right to the point.

Peter, age 1. In London 1938.
(Family photo)

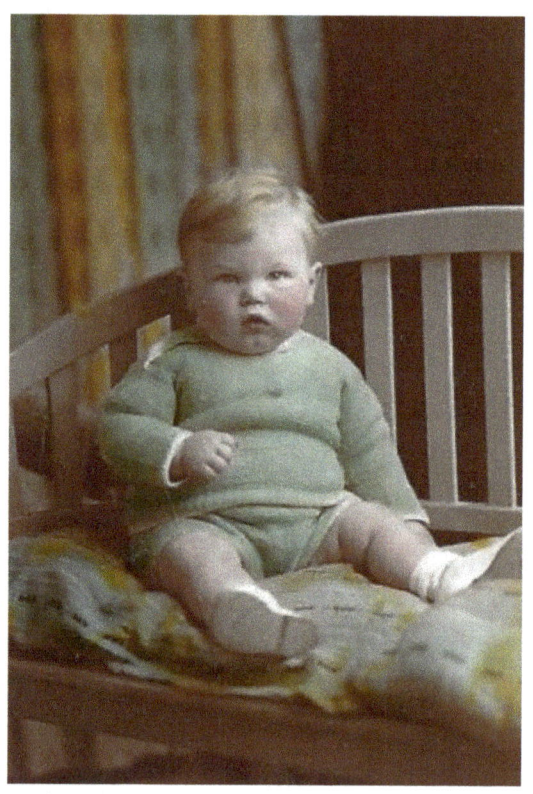

I was born on 23 February 1937. Mum and Dad were facing financial difficulties for they wanted good things for me. I was the tubbiest baby! The Royal Exchange Assurance prided itself for its social conscience so Dad asked them for a modest pay rise. The answer was 'stay as you are, or go get a job elsewhere'.

In October 1938 Dad, and two other Messenger friends, went to the RAF Balloon Recruitment Centre in London. Dad took on a 6-year contract and was 'embodied' as a Balloon Operator. The job of No1 Balloon Command was to 'sail' hundreds of balloons to form a protective 'steel curtain' around London. This was not a safe job, as we will see later!

With Dad stationed at RAF Kidbrooke in SE London, Mum wanted to be close to him, and to her parents still living with us in London. I was too young to travel so she stayed on until it became too dangerous to remain.

Evacuees leaving for a big adventure. Some liked it; others hated it.
Evacuee Memorial at the National Memorial Arboretum.
(ERA)

When war was declared in September 1939, great upheaval started. Over 250,000 children and their teachers were evacuated to safe places in just 2 weeks. Many places were not so safe, as we will see later. Younger kids usually went with their mother, as I did. Some say 120,000 evacuees came to West Sussex, with around 1200 of those sent to the Midhurst district. We will never know the real number for inadequate records were kept of who went where. My two cousins, Marjorie and Arthur Sims, were in the first wave of evacuees who came to the Midhurst area.

That number of people arriving in the District greatly overloaded accommodation, schooling, shop supplies and public services.

From September 1939, to around September 1940, Hitler directed his attention to occupying Western Europe. He would get around to taking Britain when he had Europe under his control! Few bombs were dropped on London in that period; it became known as the 'Phoney War'. Many evacuees returned to London only to return again later that year.

The 1940 summer in England was superb. Mum, still living in London, took me for picnics with friends. Dad came home on leave. All was well …. or so it seemed.

Summer 1940. Dad on leave with Peter in their London home.

The British Expeditionary Force BEF, sent to France in September 1939 to stop Hitler, was no match for his Blitzkrieg methods. The Germans did not play to the old rules of war! The miraculous Dunkirk evacuation took place in late May 1940, bringing hundreds of thousands of Allied troops back to Britain to refresh and take up the fight again.

The invasion of Britain was then a good proposition for Hitler. To begin that campaign, his Air Force tried to bomb Britain into submission. The heavy bombing Blitz on London, and elsewhere in England, began in August 1940.

Famous photo St Pauls in burning London during the 1940 Blitz.
(http://ggoofy3.tripod.com/blitz/id5.html)

I was then just 3½ years of age; old enough to see fear in others and remember it. We had an Andersen shelter dug into our London garden. Our windows were cross taped to reduce the risk of flying glass. From our front bay window, being up a hill, I laid in my cot at night watching the searchlights and distant fires glowing in central London.

The noise was horrific. Nights often had to be spent in our musty Anderson shelter waiting for the 'all clear' siren that told us it was safe to go out to see the devastation. One night a bomb demolished a complete house nearby!

That convinced Mum that it was time to evacuate! Following the advice of her sister-in-law, Aunty Lizzie Sims, we rapidly took a train to Midhurst. What luck! It turned out to a great place for me to grow up. The train, possibly from Waterloo, was full of soldiers with their rifles and kit. I carried a gas mask and had that little label attached to me that was the only record of an evacuee's movements.

Mum's home in Easebourne was the left-hand end, of the left house.
(Google Maps)

Because most of the evacuees and troops had already arrived there was no room for us to be together anywhere. Mum went to live with the Chandler's, in what is now the 'Uphams' house at the top of Easebourne Street – a TV star's house today. She became a close friend of the Chandler's daughter, Alice, of a similar age.

343 St Ann's Hill is entered in the arched porch at the left end (http://www.gravelroots.net/gallmid6g.html#2a)

I went to stay with Mrs Ena Karn at 343 St Ann's Hill in Midhurst.

Very little about my first days in Midhurst has remained in my memory. I went to preschool somewhere in the St Ann's Hill building complex – where I had the greatest creamy milk from a little, gill size, bottle.

One time, cousin Marj, being a few years older than my 4 years, took me to the Orion Cinema, (now the supermarket in North

Street), to see the latest film 'Rose Marie'. I talked so much that she did not really see the film. Looking after me made her life a bit of a misery!

St Ann's Hill path, Midhurst 1898 postcard
(www.westsussexpast.org/pictures PP/WSL/P001259 no 278)

My leisure time was spend exploring the adjacent St Ann's Hill woods and the River Bank path. I had so much freedom.

Thanks to the Sisters of the Convent they have established I went to the St Margaret's School from January 1942 to April 1943. I has sure that I was only there for a few days!

Mum would come to see me at Mrs Karn's house; to take me for a walk and play with me. At the end of these visits she would hand me back to Mrs Karn, who probably had been told to care for me, that being the requirement then. She had no children so it must have been a real upheaval of her lifestyle. The arrangement was not an easy one for anyone involved.

Boys at St Margaret's Convent School. 1940s. I could well be the lad on the left, bottom row!
(Courtesy, Convent Sisters)

Mum 'obtained' an army blanket from a friendly Canadian soldier quartermaster. With that she made me a lovely dressing gown. I was so smart. But it didn't stay with me for long. Not long after she had given it to me an Army MP arrived. He confiscated the dressing gown. For technically stealing the blanket the soldier would have been given several months of hard labour in a military prison.

The low-key life in Midhurst in 1941 was summed up by a visiting Vigilance Team, sent to see that blackouts and other war time instructions were being met. They commented that they had come to a part of England where the war had not yet arrived.

Midhurst was slow to adapt to the war. After all it must have seemed to the residents that they were so remote from the war going on elsewhere; there was little chance of being attacked by Germans.

1941 Newspaper tells it all
(Sunday Pictorial, Midhurst in Living Memory book)

SUNDAY PICTORIAL, April 8, 1941.   PAGE 5

THE MOST COCK-EYED TOWN IN BRITAIN!

BOMBS have fallen around Midhurst, in Sussex. Planes have droned overhead. But the local council does not believe in sirens.

"They disturb our sleep."

Although there is no compulsion on small towns to sound sirens, the "Sunday Pictorial" Vigilance Council finds:

That silence leads to chaos in the whole A.R.P. system.

★

TO get to Midhurst you travel on a branch line in a one-coach train.

From Midhurst Station you walk along a winding road, down a hill, over a bridge, past the Spread Eagle Hotel—and straight out of the war.

That's what it seemed like to members of the Council of Vigilance who arrived in Midhurst a few days ago.

We weren't very long in the town before we half expected to see a courier dart from one of the quaint Tudor gable-ends with the dramatic

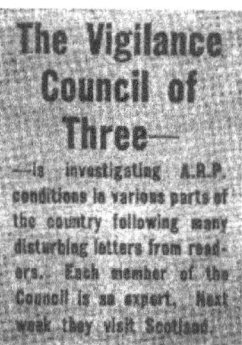

The Vigilance Council of Three

—is investigating A.R.P. conditions in various parts of the country following many disturbing letters from readers. Each member of the Council is an expert. Next week they visit Scotland.

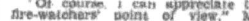

"Of course, I can appreciate the fire-watchers' point of view." Mr.

The A.R.P. people, to their credit, have tried most ways of sounding an Alert without causing a disturbance. Apart from the hand-operated siren was the horn, for instance. That was to be a siren substitute. A.R.P. officials didn't want to try it out in Midhurst itself.

Already, they considered, they were being treated like boys at play, and this would only make them a laughing stock.

So they made a discreet rendez-

When about to turn 7yrs old, on 10 February 1943, I was standing idly on the corner of the St Ann's Hill building. It was 4 40pm on a clear day. Without any warning there was a horrendous noise up at the top of Sheep Lane. All around us window glass was shattering. A huge cloud of dust arose at the top of lane. Then it all became clear.

Painting of a recently restored Dornier Do-17 bomber.
(Art Work: Hyperscale. patchesofpride.wordpress.com)

The very loud, throbbing sound of low flying aircraft engines increased. That was not heard there in normal times. A twin-engine, Dornier heavy German bomber, came by so low that I saw a crewman with his leather helmet on. It just missed hitting the church steeple as it zoomed away from the east to the west, to be gone as fast as it had come.

Piecing together several official reports made at the time, and later published memories, makes it clearer as to what had happened.

On that day several aircraft dropped bombs around the county. This bomber would have used the Bepton Road to visually navigate to the centre of the town. Approaching the corner of the Bepton and Petersfield Road corners he began to glide-bomb at a very low altitude, its bomb doors were seen to open in time for the first bomb to drop onto the Temple church. It exploded and the building was flattened. No one was killed there.

The airplane, having reached the highest point of the town, then made a circuit to the east, around the top of the Hill dropping two bombs on Sheep Lane. Many houses were damaged. One in the top road of Sheep Lane, took a direct hit: its occupants were killed. A fourth, and possibly fifth, bomb was released a fraction in time later. Due to the hill falling away in the direction of the Ruins these last bombs continued on their horizontal direction to fall harmlessly in a Cowdray Park steeplechase course.

Grave in Midhurst Cemetery of those killed during the 10 February 1943 raid on Midhurst.
(Author picture)

Evacuees from London - Peter Merrington 5yrs old, Barbara his mother, 37yrs old, and Florence Wheeler, 57yrs old - were killed as a bomb exploded right inside their cottage. Peter's father was a corporal in the RAF. To remind us of that fateful day, these three are still in Midhurst, being buried in the Cemetery.

When my mother (recall, still living in Easebourne), heard that a little boy was killed in Sheep Lane; called Peter; aged around 5; with a father, a corporal in the RAF; and all evacuees, she panicked. Surely that was me! She was so relieved when she found me safe and sound, declaring we would never live apart again.

The week of this talk is the 70th anniversary of this bombing, the only one in which life was lost by enemy action in Midhurst.

My cousin Marj was standing right by the bomb hits in Sheep Lane. She felt the blast! Her story is for another time, but suffice to say her greatest worry then was for her little yellow angora pixie hat she had left behind as she rushed from the cottage she was visiting. She wandered around asking the troops from Cowdray Park to find it for her.

Mum decided it was time for us to live together. I went to live with her in the western end of Uphams cottage at the top of Easebourne Street; it became very cramped in that 'two up and two down' cottage.

I changed schools to the Easebourne Primary School, in Easebourne Street. I have yet to identify when I started and left there; school register records appear to be lost from just before I went there.

Easebourne Primary School; now unused but looking much like it was in 1940.

(http://www.gravelroots.net/ease/easegall4k.html

My life in Easebourne was very rural. Walking up and down the street, to and from school, I passed the meadows with barbed wire defences placed up the slope to the trees along the road above.

One day I saw that he farmers were using a steam engine to thresh the grain there. The picture below is Jack Sawtell, a local. I used to play in the little cutting of a rock crusher plant by our house.

When Mum's friend, Alice, had a baby, there was insufficient space for us in our half of Uphams. We moved back into town. In Knockhundred Row we stayed in a boarding house just above the old library.

Thrashing the wheat - the old way. Note the unsafe belt on the left driving the thrasher from a steam engine. (Odhams Press, 1946.)

Living back there again, town life was also great for me. Each week I was told I could collect a Beano comic from the Newsagent in North Street.

All was not all well for Mum for she was very attractive. The landlord came on strong to her in the middle of one night, so we up and left right then; and that was in winter! It took me a while to understand why I lost my right to the comic at the newsagent: he had been paying for it.

In nearby Red Lion Street there was a tiny shop to rent, the one that was until recently Dale Baker's barber's shop, then becoming the Creative Cookies shop. It is easily recognized by the overhanging building once carrying a lion like sign in the picture below. The bracket is still there, protruding lifeless and lonely without a sign today.

Red Lion Street. The hanging sign is the building section in which the Sydenham's lived in 1943/44.
(Pathe Films, still shot, 1939)

It was far cry from the, done up, cake decoration shop fitted out in 2015. In 1943 it had a toilet and a cold water sink at the back of a small room behind the shop. A central stair-case went upstairs; there was no entrance walk-in corridor at that time as that was then part of the larger shop.

At first, we only had the ground floor. Mum put up a curtain across the room. Behind it we slept together. There was a single light globe socket in the centre of the room. To that Mum connected an electric one bar radiator. This gave us heat and was used for cooking when placed on its back on the floor.
In front of the curtain Mum did dress making – and remodelling

due to rationing. She soon obtained permission to use an upstairs room. It was cold, damp and very eerie. To make it so Dickensian the whole upstairs main room was cluttered with Victoriana stuffed fauna… insects, spiders, beetles, fish, birds and animals in glass bell jars and drawers. All were covered with decades of hanging spider webs on which dust lay.

Our shared single bed was moved upstairs into a tiny front room. To get to the room one had to navigate through a web-strewn isle without a light. Mum must have been so scared. Rats ran in the house. To me it was just another day; isn't this how everyone lived?

I roamed the district for about a 1mile radius; the distance back to home for food and sleep. I played along the river and by now, being 7yrs old, even in the running river. The South Pond marshes were also now in my range.

Lord Lovat, No 4 Commando, with others after the Dieppe Raid, August 1942.
(Wikipedia)

Soldiers were everywhere during the war period. They were camped along the Easebourne Street, above the old crusher place. The Famous No 4 Commando had its HQ in part of Cowdray House, under the command of Lord Lovat.

The Wheatsheaf Inn, between Wool Lane and North Street, Midhurst, by Adrian Hill. C.1940.

(http://collections.vam.ac.uk/item/O1023171/cowdray-ruins-midhurst-recording-britain-watercolour-hill/)

Soldiers, airmen and sailors came, from as far as Aldershot, to the local pubs, dances and to the local picture theatre. The Wheatsheaf Inn was painted in a water-colour at the time.

Tanks coming through from Petworth for D-Day (Source unclear. WSRO?)

D-Day 6th June arrived. For days before, and after, troops and materiel kept passing through to get to the South Coast .... and then it was quiet again. D-Day was not the end of hostilities by far, so troops were still around the District areas, being trained for the big push across Europe.

It was during the long summer holidays of 1944. I roamed the town taking in any excitement going.

Vengeance Bomb 1, V1. June – October 1944
(Wikipedia images)

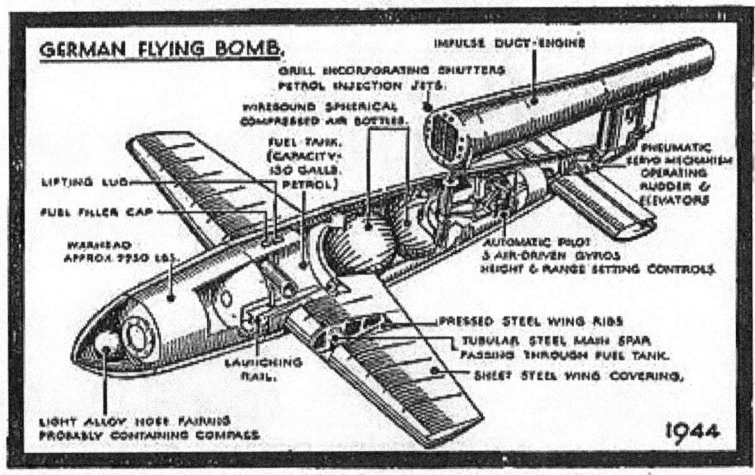

During this time Mum kept it from me that Dad had been injured at his base in RAF Kidbrooke in SE London. At 0410 hours, on 18 June 1944, a V1, 2000 lb, flying bomb made a direct hit on his hut. His right leg was seriously injured by a round 2inch diameter disc of metal shrapnel that entered his ankle and cut up in his leg bone.

In the 1960's, he told me a little of what had happened. He was the only person of his hut that was not killed. He would have missed injury at all if he had not put out his leg to get down from his bunk. Where this happened is now a community allotment.

At the time there was no chance of visiting him in the Brook Hospital, next to Kidbrooke, as it was in the centre of the V weapon targets.

Kidbrooke Park Allotment. Spot where RAF Cpl Sydenham's Hut took a direct hit by a V1 bomb in June 1944.
(Courtesy Kidbrooke Park Allotment Association. 2013

Mum eventually told me he had been hurt after he had been transferred, on 6 July, to convalesce in the Royal West Sussex hospital. We went to see him in the grounds of the hospital.

Sometime during this period, I was down on the meadows of the causeway when I heard military brass and pipe bands in the distance. I rushed to see what it was. There was a magnificent military parade passing up North Street. I do not have a photo of it: you have to use your imagination.

Example Scottish pipe band at Canongate. Edinburgh 2009

(http://en.wikipedia.org/wiki/File:Pipe_band_in_the_Canongate_Edinburgh.jpg)

It may have been the 'Salute to Soldiers' week held in Midhurst to raise funds for the still continuing war effort. Columns of troops and vehicles, interspersed with bands, passed by me. What an inspiring show!

Also, perhaps at that time, I stumbled on a fund-raising fete in the

Cowdray Ruins grounds. I wandered in, out, and about with no one seemingly noticing me; just another evacuee on the loose.

Several huge tents had displays of army and paratrooper gear. Army stunts were being performed. Most interesting were the yellow runner blow-ups moored on the river, one each side of the causeway bridge. People were asked to throw a coin into them from the bridge. Swimmers would dive for coins that missed the dinghies, as most did….. purposefully! Perhaps one day someone, with waterproof metal detector, will find coins missed by the divers and thereby prove my memory was correct. No one seems to know of it happening!

The Fitz Hall Gate Lodge as it is today, much larger.
(Own photo)

Dad was discharged from the Royal Chichester Hospital on 29 September 1944. He was given a week's leave before reporting to a new post in Blackpool on 4 October. Mum and Dad went away for the week leaving me to stay with Auntie Lizzie then living in the gate house of Fitz Hall.

That was yet another adventure. It was even worse a place to live than where Mum and I were in Red Lion Street. The Sims family, however, had found a place that let them live together again. It had no running water; one winched up water from a well outside the back door. There was no electricity; light came from smelly oil lamps. The toilet was a 'long drop' in a hut, down the back garden. Heating was from the kitchen wood stove. But they were enjoyable days. We kids slept together in a bed with a colourful patchwork quilt; made from left-over squares of rationed and old materials.

For me things were getting better. I then had my two cousins to play with. We were in an interesting area with its large sand pits, remote Home Guard hut, pine forest, and rhododendron woods.

Painting by an unknown artist depicts a V-E Day celebration between Yanks and Brits in England.
(http://www.skylighters.org/veday2004/)

The last of the larger, V2 Vengeance rockets, dropped on London on 27 March 1945. There was no longer any significant German capability to drop bombs, or fly rockets. The Allies were pushing on well to silence Germany.

The war in Europe ended on 7 May 1945; *'Victory in Europe'* VE day.

I have no idea when we left the Red Lion Street shop and returned to London, but I think it was before VE day. Going back to what was left intact in our London home, left unoccupied for the war period, Mum, Dad and I entered home again. There was no electricity available so Dad lit the gas light on the wall… a left over from the Victorian era, still useful in an emergency.

It was a time of wonderful peace, but much austerity. Dad was retraining as a structural steel draftsman, still with his gammy leg wound. Money was short. Rationing was still on. All along the streets were bombed-out houses. The country had enormous debt.

Peter, with Mum and Dad (LHS), arrive in Adelaide in 1951.

Dad's two sisters in Adelaide, Australia had married WW1 Australian soldiers. Letters came that wrote of cream by the pint, exotic fruit falling from their trees and freedom to build your own home on your own large plot of land. There was little rationing in Australia and most families even had a motor car. On top of that Adelaide was situated by fabulous beaches which saw much sun and little rain for months on end. Dad applied to be sponsored migrants on the £10 pom scheme!

In October 1951 we entered Australia; my evacuee story behind me.

Earlier, I hinted that Cowdray Hall is a special spot for me. For the annual concert of St Margaret's primary school, it must have been around 1942, I was a key performer in a short skit about Wee Willie Winkle. I was lying in a bed up on the stage that existed then.

Cowdray Hall today. Peter was in a school concert here c1942. (http://www.cowdrayhall.co.uk/gallery)

When Wee Willie knocked on the window, to enquire if I was asleep, I was supposed to rattle a spoon in a jug on the floor. The time came. I reached out for the spoon. The prompter person whispered *"rattle the spoon"*. Nothing was heard! She prompted again, and again, getting louder each time. Eventually I whispered back, very loudly, *"I can't reach!"*

The audience of locals and soldiers laughed, and laughed, as the curtain fell. (I do not know if Inspector Christopher Foyle was in that audience!).

You probably guessed. That hall was then the Easebourne Village Institute, this very place. I was back again!

So, we come to the end of the main thread of the 'story line' of my memories. I am now researching and adding the back story to fill in the account as the life and times of WW2 Midhurst, not just mine.

Several key dates and physical items are still missing. What was that army parade? When was that Fete held? Where are the artefacts left behind that tell us the soldiers were actually here? What was going on in the HQ of No 4 Commando under Lord Lovat? Where did we kids go to be isolated when a chicken pox epidemic struck town?

My visit there in that February 2014 was to research the local records and talk to residents for accounts of these, and other events.

This following artwork, done around 1890 in the Convent Community, parallels my work. Midhurst and Easebourne gave me my childhood formation experiences that I will give back in my memoirs project.

St Margaret's Convent work of c1890s.
(Convent of Mercy, Midhurst)

Thank you all for listening. I hope, for many of the older folks, these memories will trigger yours.

To those who did not experience the WW2 state of affairs this might encourage them to look toward peace, and be prepared to work hard to keep it.

Regretfully, there is a major lack of photos and artefacts of the WW2 Midhurst District. It has sometimes been necessary to use images that represent the events instead.

Readers who can help with their experiences can contact mw, Peter Sydenham on Sydenham@senet.com.au.

Appreciations

I wish to thank those who have given this project a flying start with their important local publications. These include the several 'memories' books produced in recent times for Midhurst, Easebourne, Fernhurst, The Hartings and Cocking.

The West Sussex Record Office is a most important and valuable facility. Frances Lansley has been so helpful there.

Appreciation is also due to many local residents who have given their time to assist my enquiries, most notable being Sue Edwards, Tania Pons, Jean Piggott and Andrew Guyatt.

Assistance of the *Midhurst and Petworth Observer* newspaper is acknowledged, the key contact having been then Ellie Evans.

The Internet, with its Wikipedia contributors, has provided an enormous boost to the way historical research can now be carried out.

What that lecture started

With these events now presented you too, may be wanting to know what went on as the back stories of that time.

That pull on me to better understand, and thus really appreciate, those traumatic times was the reason I began to collect material on the life and times of the small, 110square mile, Midhurst Rural District. If something had a war time link to the area it was collected.

Looking around for already published accounts on the WW2 period showed that little had been recorded about the Midhurst District, it presumably, not attracting interest because of it smallness in the general scheme of things in areas, such as West Sussex. I expected to find little that would be of real interest.

As the following years from 2014 – 2017 progressed I was much surprised to find numerous events and lives that were as exciting as a fiction thriller. These were often not on-line, but found in books well out-of-print. A book collection has been built up from books and regenerated on-line older books dating back to the 18th century. The collection has some 300 items in it.

Out of that was born the Midhurst WW2 Memoirs project – see www.midhurstmemoirs.com

The Book Series

We are all part of our past.
You can't do anything - write a poem or make a pudding -
Without reference to past skills, past experience, past attitudes
And we are right to show affection
To what others before us have achieved ....
Not just because they are familiar or beautiful
Or part of our history,
But because they help to give us a sense of place,
A sense of our identity and thus can be reassuring.
                                                    Sir Lewis Casson.

Clearly what I had to provide as my contribution was a readable, story-like, account. My own evacuee story line rapidly became the sparse thread upon which to attach the many back stories.

What did a WW1 V.C. medal winner have to do with my morning milk drink in kindy? What had one of villages of the area have to do with the start of the Modern Art genre? Who gave Joyce the name of Lord Haw-Haw? And many more!

The overall result is a kind of penetrating anthology that encapsulates the history of the Midhurst District up to the 1950s.

The *Midhurst WW2 Memoirs* material now collected, will need several books to deal with its depth. It will cover the resources as:

Period 1 Pre-war (Pre1940)

Period 2 Lowest Times (1940-1942)

Period 3 Fight Back (1943-mid 1944)

Period 4 Peace Returns (mid 1944-1950)

Period 1 comprises:

Book 1: ***Midhurst WW2 Memoirs: 1. A Place Close to My Heart.***

Book 2. ***Midhurst WW2 Memoirs: 2. Nazis Storm Clouds -1930s.***

Book 3. ***Midhurst WW2 Memoirs: 3. The District Responds.***

Book 1: *Midhurst WW2 Memoirs: 1. A Place Close to My Heart.*

(Release Date. April 2018)

Rear Cover Page:

'A region of picturesque and sylvan beauty that I have never seen equalled.' - Benjamin Disraeli. 1870.

By British town standards, Midhurst in West Sussex, was always a sleepy place, becoming that way due to its enviable geographical position in award-winning rural countryside. WW2 filled it with troops and evacuees.

In readiness for the war time memoirs to come, this first book, of a series on Midhurst during WW2, tells of interesting happenings as it delves into the back stories of the area's history. Extensive research and scholarly professionalism by Peter Sydenham integrates a surprising amount of 'all but lost' material, showing its place in helping win that war and how 'it is a place to be'. You will enjoy learning about the Midhurst District and its WW2 endurance.'

Book 2. *Midhurst WW2 Memoirs: 2. Nazis Storm Clouds - 1930s.*

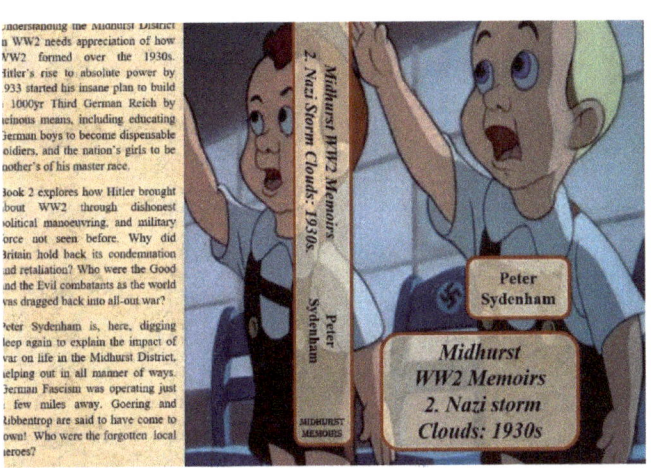

(Release Date. Late 2018)

Rear Cover Page:
Understanding the Midhurst District in WW2 needs appreciation of how WW2 formed over the 1930s. Hitler's rise to absolute power by 1933 kick-started his insane plan to build a 1000yr Third German Reich by heinous means, including educating German boys to become dispensable soldiers, and the nation's girls to be mothers of his master race.

Book 2 explores how Hitler brought about WW2 through dishonest political manoeuvring, and military force not seen before. Why did Britain hold back its condemnation and retaliation? Who were the Good and the Evil combatants as the world was dragged back into all-out war?
Peter Sydenham is, here, digging deep again to explain the impact of war on life in the Midhurst District. Fascism was operating just a

few miles away. Goering and Ribbentrop are said to have come to town! Who were the local infamous Nazis; and forgotten local heroes?

Book 3 *Midhurst WW2 Memoirs:* 3. The District Responds.

Release Date: mid 2019

Synopsis:
War is imminent at the start of 1939. Preparations are underway that take away much freedom of living in the District. Young men are called up. Rationing is introduced. Permission is needed to use a motor vehicle. Houses must be blacked out. Pilots are training to repel the German Air Force. Evacuees and troops fill every place of accommodation. Life is undergoing a major trauma.

(The remaining books have their contents selected and ordered. All material is held in e-file form. This project has, apart from the book collection, little paper record. It is first assembled into books using the writer's tool, *Scrivener.)*

www.ingramcontent.com/pod-product-compliance
Lightning Source LLC
Chambersburg PA
CBHW062106290426
44110CB00022B/2730